WOKE

A POETIC JOURNEY

BY: SHARRAN C. TAYLOR

A.K.A. KWEEN YAKINI

Copyright © by Sharran C. Taylor

All rights reserved.

ISBN-13: 978-1732371002

ISBN-10: 1732371008

DEDICATION

I am especially dedicating this book to my mother Catherine and my daughter Christina. And my sincere appreciation to everyone who has supported me along this journey.

INTRODUCTION

WOKE is my 1st published collection of poetry, and it tells a story about my self-reflecting journey. WOKE is a term that means to be fully aware of one's self and one's surroundings. However, I spent a large part of my life being unhappy and I couldn't understand why. But, it was my unhappiness that lead me to question my path. It forced me to step back and examine my life, and it made me accept responsibility for my unhappiness. This is when I realized that I was going to have to make some significant changes in my life, starting with myself. Fortunately, I was able to find my way back to my center, and gradually I started becoming the woman I was meant to be. Through some deep soul searching and research, I learned how to expand my thoughts. My new perspectives then allowed me to write with a depth, clarity and insight that I had never known. Now I am honored to be able to share my personal journey with you.

TABLE OF CONTENTS

OBLIVION

PIECES OF ME	6
MY SISTAH'S KEEPER	9
A FALLEN STAR	11
YOUNG KING, YOUNG KING	13
MENTAL SLAVES	15
AMERICAN PIE	16
REAL AS FUCK	18

ANCESTOR'S SONG

MY ALKEBULAN (AFRICA)	22
BLACK SOLDIERS SOUL	24
BLACK GOLD	25
A TIME	27
WE ARE THE GREAT	28
THE SLAVE TRADE	30
UNTOLD STORY	32
I AM HERE BELOVEDS	34

BOLD AND BEAUTIFUL

OUR BLACKNESS	38
I AM THE SHIT	39
SPITTING FIRE	42
NO RAVING BEAUTY	44
BLACK AND BROWN GIRLS	45
THE ORIGINAL WOMBMAN	46
BLACK MOTHERS	47
BLACK LOVE	50

NOW I SEE

FEAR VS PEACE	54
BONES IN THE CLOSET	55
THE VALUE OF TIME	57
THE DIRTY, DIRTY	60
ONE OF BROOKLYN'S FINEST	63
BACK IN MY DAY	66

SOCIAL CONSCIOUSNESS

I GOT SOMETHING TO SAY!	70
BLACK AND BLUE	72
MESSAGE VIRAL	74
CHOICES	76
FEARSOME TIMES	77
TOO BLACK	79
BLACK LIPS	80
BLACK SKIN	82
WHAT ABOUT US?	83
FAKE DEMOCRACY	84
IDENTITY STOLEN	86
WORLD OF "INSTAGRAM"	87

SPIRITUAL AWAKENING

RESTORATION OF MY SOUL	90
WHO AM I	92
ILLUSION OF PERFECTION	94
COSMIC PERCEPTIONS	96
SEEING BEYOND 20-20	97
THE GOD'S CHILD	98
ANCIENT WINDS	100

WOKE

CONFESSIONS	104
FUCK MEDIOCRITY	106
I DO THIS FOR MY PEOPLE	108
FOR THE R.B.G.	110
MY TRUTH IS DOPE	112
TRUTH PILL	113
HELLA FOCUSED	115
THE TRUTH	117

OBLIVION

PIECES OF ME

I am a collage of pieces
    That can show you a different picture
    Depending on how you look at me
You see, some of my pieces are good
    But some pieces are twisted
    And some of my pieces
    Just don't ever seem to fit together

There are pieces of me
That sometimes conform into
A dangerous concoction
Of unequal parts
Shaken, stirred and poured
Into a slightly chipped cocktail glass
That should come with a caution label like:
    "Warning consumption of this individual may cause side effects"
    Because I do have trouble keeping my emotions in check
    And I do pay more attention to the size of a man's paycheck
    So I'll put his love on lay away
    And ask him if I can take a range check
    Because he doesn't know that my self-esteem is too low
    For me to have self-respect
But wait
I digress
Because I need to stitch these pieces together
And dissect
The good from the bad

I really need to give myself a make over
From this lifestyle fad
And stop fantasizing
About what I never had
Because this shell of a life is too fucking sad
    Sometimes I laugh at myself
    Because I can't even get mad
But now that I'm ready
    I don't even know where to start
And I think my percentage is about
    70% bad parts
With all the pain
    Misleading love games
    And forgotten names
All the who, what, when and why's
    And the many nights I've cried
Because none of my wishes
    Seem to be coming true
And I've tried to stop wishing
    But my desires keep insisting
And I guess in life sometimes
    We all gotta settle
I should know
I'm an expert
    And they need to give me a medal
    For being the best sucker of the year!
See how my self-worth just disappears
    And I can shift through levels of pain like gears

So fuck it
    I'm ready to do whatever it takes!
Like the way I use to give it up on first dates
Like I've been played so many times
    My middle name should be Check Mate!
But I'm getting my shit together
    And I'll be like that

Six Million Dollar Woman
As soon as I figure out how to rearrange these pieces
So that I can become my better version
I'll be more confident
And More Beautiful
Like no other version of me ever existed

But I'll still just be a collage of pieces
That can show you a different picture
Depending on how you look at me
You see, some of my pieces are good
But some pieces are twisted
And some of my pieces
Just don't ever seem to fit together

MY SISTAH'S KEEPER

She's keeps looking for respect
    Out there in those streets
Hoping to find a King
    That she can't seem to meet

She hates all the lies
    And being treated like a stone
Being cast away
    Like she's not a treasure to own

And she is the mother of the earth
    Yet she's living in despair
Struggles with the color of her skin
    And hates her natural hair

She says my lips are too full
And my hips are too wide
And my butt is too big
    For a model's size

She can't see her worth
    And that she is a Queen
All the men try to holla
    They say Girl
    Why are you looking so mean?"

They say I'm digging ya walk
    With those sexy dark thighs
They lower her thoughts
    Because sex is the prize

They spit a good game
>   Trying to sell her a dream
They say I need you Queen
>   To be on my team

She turns her head
>   'Cause it sounds good in her ear
But I say don't fall for it sistah
>   For you'll awake in tears

My Sistah I will protect you
>   From those slippery words
For I have the wisdom
>   That you have yet to learn

I tell you the secret
>   About your DNA
She looks at me funny
>   And asks what did you say?

I say, It's true my sistah
>   You are divine and all
But if you follow that path
>   You are sure to fall

But I am my sistah's keeper
>   And you are me
And we are one under the sun
>   For all eternity

So, I will teach you
>   For you are my equal
But today my sistah
>   I just want to reach you

A FALLEN STAR

She's a commissioned pleasure
A fallen star
Sometimes she strips in bars
With beautifully hidden scars

Hustling is her game
But you don't know her pain
There are so many who have
Id's with fake names

She moves in the haunting lights
Customers pay her for the night
Tall, sensual and lean
Not as friendly as she seems

She's street bred
With an empty canvas in her head
She works from her bed
'Cause that's how she's fed

Her type breeds infection
They despise his erections
You better use protection
Consequences need injections

She never learned how to read
Never has her body been pleased
Routinely checked for disease
But if she dies will you grieve?

She's living a dual reality
But what if she could see
Beyond this actuality
Who else could she be?

Her anguish is so profound
Yet you keep passing her around
Like a joint you found
When will you see the queen inside
With the invisible crown

Notice the sorrow in her eyes
Unleash her silent cries
It doesn't matter how or why
She needs her chance to fly

Set her up on a throne
Give her a place to call home
Treat her like one of your own
And tell her she's not alone

Do not dismiss her
Be her gentle kisser
She could have been your sister
So, please help her mister!

YOUNG KING, YOUNG KING

There's a war going on
      In my back yard every night
And I can't stand no more of this death and dying
So, can I speak with you for a minute!
Can you please just stop and listen!

Young King, Young King!
Have you lost your crown?
      It seems that it's nowhere to be found

Are you killing time?
Or is time killing you?
      'Cause it seems like you all dying except for a few
I keep seeing blood spatter
      Exploding like self-destructive matter
But all you seem to care about
      is keeping those pockets fatter

I see you running so fast
As life keeps flowing pass
      But I see no future for you in the looking glass

Young King, Young King
Where is your crown?
Did you leave it in the lost and found?
He said it's long gone now!
I said well that don't surprised me somehow
      'Cause you gave these streets your vow
      And left your son a fatherless child!

And this situation is all too common here
On these streets I see you disappear
Mothers keep losing their sons to fear
One more warrior killed by the spear

And I see you chilling at the same old spot
    But you gotta run out the back
    Before they unload that Glock
    Before they call the cops
I know these streets are hot
    But statistics say that
    You might get shot

Young King, Young King
    Please pick up your crown
    'Cause I get sad when I see you just hanging around
You keep sending your brothers to an early grave
    Since you're A king by blood
    I guess that makes you a royal slave
Another early deceased
Another a prince lost in these streets
Tell me what happened to the king
Who you were born to be!

MENTAL SLAVES

They said look at those niggas over there
      they think they've got it good
But just look at how they're living
      in those slummy neighborhoods

They said we see y'all spending all your money
      buying the latest smart phones and whips
But why some of you can't afford to leave
      the waitress a decent tip?
Maybe you should just take a seat at the bar
      order one drink and slowly sip

They said we see y'all got them fancy jewels and all that bling
      But y'all look so ridiculous with those platinum coated things
Maybe that's why you can't afford to marry your girlfriend
      and buy her and engagement ring
Because y'all niggas are just too busy
      pretending like you've got everything

They said, y'all only live for thrills
      maybe that's why you can't afford to pay all your bills
Yet some of you think that you're too good to shop at the Goodwill

They said yes, we gave you your freedom
      but we can tell that your mind is still locked
They said we heard you got big plans
      but that's funny because we never see you leave your block!

AMERICAN PIE

Yeah, they gone make you crawl
for that American Dollar
So much greed it makes
a poor man wanna Holla
And most folks are just barely getting by
And won't even get a sliver of that American Pie
before they die!

So, let me breakdown the situation
'cause we not trying to hear the media's explanation
talking about this is a Fox News Investigation
and then they ask you about your political affiliations
so they can pimp you for campaign donations
Then they change their position after the inauguration
And turn around and create more economic inflation

And some might think that this is an exaggeration
but the reason why the police
want to increase the population
of these Prison Plantations
is so that after the incarceration
they can withhold the voter registration

And it's not just a coincidence why
they underfund our children's education
and why they classify our racial denomination
so that they can justify our lower salary compensation
or deny our employment applications
      due to some technical disqualification

And the problem just ain't one
thing but a combination,
and here's some news

that might be ground breaking,
did you know that free knowledge
is yours for the taking?
but it starts with a collaboration of conscious
elevation

'Cause they gone make you crawl for that American Dollar
So much greed makes a poor man wanna Holla
And most folks are barely just getting by
And won't even get a sliver of that American Pie
before they die!

REAL AS FUCK

I'm about to get real as fuck!
Sometimes we act like crabs in a bucket
Yeeah, I said it
    so, fuck it
But there is a reason why
    we be hating on each other
    and why we can't seem to love one another
A reason why we walk by and don't even speak
    and then go to church and preach
    about turning the other cheek
I say it's time to find a cure
    for this disease called Willie Lynch
'Cause that Stockholm Syndrome
    must be got y'all convinced
It's time to break the chains
    on this Jim Crow Hold
'Cause we helped build this shit
    So, this is our home
Can't you all see that this affliction
    is nothing more than a
    post traumatic slavery condition
And that's why some brothers
    will date any other race
    except for the one
    with their mother's face
    And it's so sad to see
    but they must have forgotten
    that it was a Queen
    who helped them pick that cotton

But they say all we need
    is a good Job
    with good benefits
    and good pay

    and a good relationship
    so, we can fuck all this stress away!
But let's get back to the story
    of how many remain in poverty
    while just a few get all the glory
Now ain't that a trip?
They believe that they are the shit
    just because their ancestors came here by choice
    and ours came on the bottom of slave ships
But the truth be told
    everything they have they stole
And what they couldn't steal
    they made us build
    against our will
Yeah, we demanded reparations
    because it was time to pay that bill
But there are serious repercussions
    that we need to be discussing
    about the Black Family's
    social and economic destruction
And if all this deceit ain't enough
    now they want to GMO our food
    and contaminate our water
Yeah, the wolf is always trying to
    kill the sheeps in a slaughter
And some of y'all might not make it
    if you keep trying to fit in
    and trying to fake it

And don't drink that tea
    'cause I think they laced it
This system is a trap
    you better Get Out!
    of this Matrix
These problems are real
    better wake up this ain't no illusion

time for us to stop all this confusion
so, this is my contribution
I'm gone be part of the solution
help rid our minds of the pollution
I'll call it a consciousness revolution
I'm doing my part
to give the next generation the facts
so that hopefully one day our people
can get their greatness back!

ANCESTOR'S SONG

MY ALKEBULAN (AFRICA)
Note: The ancient name of Africa was Alkebulan Which in Arabic means "The Mother of Mankind"

Dear Ancient Africa
My Alkebulan
A coal miner's dream
See her fruitful diamonds flourish
Like a running stream
See how their sweat rolls down
And drip from their brows
As they tirelessly dig,
and they plow
To steal the wealth of Mother Africa
Yesterday and Now
With beautiful hues of color
Some subtle and some bold
Her African seeds are so fertile
She spouts pebbles of gold
And it truly is an amazing display
Of beauty to behold
But too many riches
Corrupt a weak man's soul
My Alkebulan is plush with minerals
From A to Z
They come for all her treasures
From Sea to Sea
Dark Rich Kemet Soil
Filled with an abundance
Of precious black oil
And pirate hands will chafe
As they watch and toil
Waiting for our beautiful black flesh to spoil

She is mother Alkebulan

adorned with Cocoa beans
and Tropical fruits
bursting with delicious nectar
down to her roots
But in that sacred land
their elders will live
a long life of Youth
Entrusted to pass on
Mother Africa's Ancient Truth

A BLACK SOLDIERS SOUL

I feel the restless souls
Of our soldiers taken
I grieve for you
My heart never stops breaking
I hear your silent screams
And your unconscious rest seeking explanation
For your immoral and premature termination
Your light was stolen by a racist's perpetration

I feel your pain and forever I mourn
I feel your hunger for revenge
I know that you have been eternally scorned
Truly you have been greatly wronged
And your sacred flesh should never have been torn

But the fight for justice still remains
And we will carry on
Have no fear beloved
For there will be another dawn
Listen for the trumpet of the Ancestors horn
And Rest in Power good soldier
Once again you will be reborn

BLACK GOLD

She is that Black Gold, What?
She is that Black Gold, who?
She is Black Gold
    One of the greatest treasure they ever stole
    Enslaved Cargo bought and sold
    She is Black gold on slave ships sailed
    They displayed her body like goods on sale
    Yet Black Gold still prevailed
    And here she is to tell her tale
She be that Black Gold, What?
She be that Black Gold, who?
    Mastered the Underground Railroad
    Rocking them exotic Cornrows
    The real story is still untold
    See our legacy start to unfold
We be that Black Gold, what?
We be that Black Gold, who?
    We be those Old Souls
    And, we shine like Indigo
    And, we climb his totem pole
    And, she's your Best Homie when it's time to roll
    And, we live by a different code
Yeah, we be that Black Gold, what?
We be that Black Gold, who?
    Designed by the creator in Solid Form
    Cut from a different cloth, we ain't the norm
    We ride his surf board in the early morn
    We laugh at bullshit like man come on
She be that Black Gold, What?
She be that Black Gold, who?
    We all know that Black Gold don't crack
    Our shades can range from light to black
    We got Big Afros with tattoos on our backs
    One taste and you're hooked

                now you can't go back
She be that Black Gold, What?
She be that Black Gold, who?
      She'll turn his house in to a home
      She'll turn that skin in to solid stone
      She'll break him down to the wish bone
      Her Almond Oiled skin is too slick to hold
We be that Black Gold, what?
We be that Black Gold, who?
      We be dranking that Black Tea
      And, we be toking that good Weed
      And, we carry that Essential Seed
      And, I be that dope ecstasy
      'Cause I gotta have a King next to me
      Talking that mental sex to me
She be that Black Gold, What?
She be that Black Gold, who?
      She always keeps that Yoni tight
      You wanna make her your wife
      But here's a little advice
      Learn to speak once but listen twice
      'Cause Black Gold's a winner now roll the dice!
She be that Black Gold, what?
She be that Black Gold, who?
      We be that Black Gold, Yeah
      We be that Black Gold!

A TIME

Close your eyes and let me take you there
Can you feel the Ancestors' spirit in the air?
Now let me open your thoughts to a different time
A time before man made religion
A time before racial divisions
A time where no truth was hidden
A time where we all had 3rd vision

Back to a time when we lived so natural and free
When we lived near pyramids governed by majesties'
When we strived to live like royalty
When reaching your highest self was the epitome
And where they created the first University

If you close your eyes, you can almost see
A time when life & death was a celebration
A time when we all had conscious elevation
A time when there was no mass incarceration
And a time when there was no need for emancipation
And no need to receive reparations
A time before colonization
A time before slavery plantations
And constitutional proclamations
A time when we lived in harmony without segregation
A time when we healed ourselves with Holistic
    Medication
When we respected the Laws of Nature
When we lived by the principles of MAAT Justification
Because there once was a time when one set of laws
    governed our nation

WE ARE THE GREAT

All bare witness thy kingdom will come!
For we are the seeds of the ancient ones
The architects of the Great Sphinx
The originators of Egyptian Ink
In search of the missing Link
We pay homage to our ancestors
Wiped out by an enemy
Gone in the span of a blink
They were the magnificent and transcendent Egyptians
Their evidence is written in Hieroglyphic Encryptions
We honor the Original Masters of Description

All bare witness thy kingdom will come!
I bring this message to the children of the sun
Continue to keep your heads held high
Even though the truth they falsify
Yet we can see a future of Golden Rings
For Black Men will gain power upon remembering
All behold the rise of the Warrior King
No, we will not rest until our royalty is once again seated
So, you may dismiss those history books
Where the truth has been deleted

All bare witness thy kingdom will come!
The prophecy says that we must become one
We must Elevate our kind
We must Emancipate our minds
We must forget about the fallacy of Sins
So, we can feel a shift in the wind
So, we can watch a new reality unfold
Where our crowns will be adorned
with precious crystals and gold
Where enlightened Kings and Queens will begin to rise

Learning to live like Gods without paying those tithes
Because God is already in you
So, there ain't no saints sitting in them pews
We shall see the righteous become many
and the wicked become few
Let us all bare witness when thy kingdom comes!

THE SLAVE TRADE

They came baring shiny trinkets and gifts
They came on the "Good Jesus Ship"
They said that they wanted to make a trade
But the plan was to create an international market
    off the backs African Slaves
Universal Law tells us that
    this wicked debt must be paid
For all the souls that Mother Africa gave
The slaves that created the currency
    for the New European Age
Is the same gold that gives value to our
    currency of today
And that gold should've had the names
    of the African people engraved
For the Mother land was stripped of everything
    and its people were betrayed
They were led astray by naive Kings
Indeed, a price was paid for such terrible things
But quietly do winds blow when our
Ancestor's spirits sing
About a treacherous past that continues to sting

Respectfully heads must bow
    at the millions of souls lost
To build up the new land
    at such a Bloody Cost

Slave ships contaminate their countries flags
And if we dare to speak of their route to power
    then our words might be gaged
For they are now engrained with bloodstains
And the haunting past of history will remain
Though righteous men will acknowledge

      all the suffering and pain
But they will live with the burden
      that it was their Ancestors
Who carried the African people here in chains

UNTOLD STORY

She thinks she's invisible
but you could never miss her
So I'm telling the untold story
of one of my sistahs
They say that she was blacker than black
When she tried to run away
they whipped her on her back
She was abused and used by many
Her master use to take her around back
to give her plenty
But she never knew lovin'
Because to him
she wasn't nothing!
Without being the least aware
she walks with swagger
Her heart is so heavy
she dreams of killing it with a dagger
"Chile you sho is slow
go and fetch me some water
Better close your ears
because those pigs are about to get slaughtered"
Those poor little pigs, yes indeed
She thinks lucky for them
But I wish it was me
She say's, "now let me get on down this road
I got plenty of walking to do
so just leave me alone"
She carries her head so low
She just wants to disappear from this lousy life
When she turns 15 they say
she might make a half decent wife
'Cause she's just another nigga child
Just another mouth they have to feed
They say if she has her cycle and bleeds

then it's time to make her breed
Yet my sister keeps on praying
for this cold world to change
But before that day comes
She'll die in them chains

I AM HERE BELOVEDS

I've come for you beloveds
But you must keep reaching
Yes, I know it's been grueling and hard
like the skin on your back
Tainted with scars
Like the aching
in the pit of your stomach
for our suffering to be disbarred
So no longer can we wait
For salvation from God

Our souls are yearning for peace
like a mirage in the sands
     so you must
Run!
Climb!
Crawl if you can!
     to find refuge
in this malicious land
A place where there will be
no more chains
and no more whips
and we will exorcise the demons
of those slave ships
Let our journey to liberation
be noted in scripts
even if I must grip
the bones off your finger tips
I will do whatever it takes
I won't let you slip
Here I am beloveds
reach up high
and on our ancestor's wings

we all shall fly
And with all my heart
I curse those shackles
put upon you
by those human jackals
Keep on reaching
I know we'll prevail this time
our descendants lead the way
I can see the path in my mind
We must keep moving on
no matter how great the storms
pushing through high bushes and lethal thorns
we are taking the trail before the light of dawn
so the tyrants won't know
that we are already gone
Follow the light Beloveds
for its only you that I revere
so have no fear
through our blessings
their Karma will appear
Let my knees and arms be bent
let every drop of my courage be spent
for one day they shall repent
Hear me now beloved!
Yes, I have a message to preach
there is a new horizon within our reach
and all their illusions we will breach
and future generations we will teach
and one day they will deliver
      our victory speech!

BOLD AND BEAUTIFUL

OUR BLACKNESS

Our black coilly hair
Our full coco lips
Our thick comforting thighs
And our wide swaying hips

Our hypnotizing walk
Our delicious skin tones
Our genetic divinity
And the invisible crown on our domes

Our ancestor's spirit
Our royal birthright
Our elevated consciousness
And our affinity to the sunlight

Our fearless nature
Our protective hearts
Our yearning for knowledge
And our flames lighting the dark

I AM THE SHIT

Every day I tell myself
That I am the shit!
That I am the
Shizel, Forizel my Nizel!
But I'll hold you down
With the weight of my crown
You see my honor is etched in stone
That's why they call me Goddess of the throne
Because I am the shit!
The way I dog pound it
The way I made him cum
'Cause I licked around it
And when I walk into a room
That shit gets lit!
But maybe you can't feel me
'Cause my thoughts sneak up on you
Like a Hurricane right before it hits
Yeah, I'm the shit
And not just because of the way I spit
Even though I only gave you just a little bit
Though I do keep my circle smaller
Then I keep my click
And they found evidence of our existence
Carved in ancient clay
Our History was white washed
Yet we still lived to see another day
And I make them heads turn my way
When I walk with that sway
Probably because I just got my hair
And nails done that day
You see Men wanna buy me drinks
But I wanna make men think
And I would rather wear black
Than be pretty in pink

But on a Friday night
Sometimes I'll flirt with a Wink
Yeah I'm the shit
But a fight with you I'll never pick
Because Brotha I came to build with you
And be real with you
I didn't come here to watch Netflix
And chill with you
Brotha, that ain't what we Queen's do!
You see, we keep it 100 proof
We carry the seeds that become the youth
And we keep holding on like your last tooth
I said I am
What I am
What I am
Got Damn!
I'm The Queen you see protesting
And taking a stand
I'm the right hand
Of the Black Man
Our bond is deeper than oil
found in the African Sand
I am Diamonds
I am Pearls
I am Rubies !
And yes I'm all that
Like Grandma's Easter Sunday Hat

Yeah I'm the shit!
Like Fried Chicken
Collard Greens
Corn Bread
Yams
And Smoked Lima Beans
I'm the shit!
Like that good morning sex

When I know his shit is erect
So I ride him so good and
And he gets up early to make me breakfast

Oh Yeah, that's how you'll know
That I am the shit!

SPITTING FIRE

I got 99 problems
But being Black ain't one
I got melanin rich skin
That can absorb the sun
I'm quicker than your blade
My thoughts will leave you in the shade
Don't ever try to control me
Just love and hold me
My moods might get nasty
So just keep looking pass me
I'm more than strong
Because my wisdom is so long
This sounds like a melody
Maybe I should write a song
I feel my Chakra getting higher
So let me spit this fire
I'm growing daily
So my words can't fail me
Now if you say trust me
And always saying that you love me
Then hold me down
and put no one above me!
Yeah know I wanted to let you hit that
Wanted to let you lick and flip that
But you couldn't excite my Yoni
'Cause Yo Ass was too phony
Guess I gotta play with myself
If I get too lonely
Yeah I know my flow keeps changing
And my thoughts keep rearranging
So I'm gonna slow it down a bit
'Cause I got this joint that I'm about to hit
What's my prescription?
My medicine is weed!

It keeps my energy high and satisfies my need
Alright just chill 'cause I'm about to leave
But I hope this fire I spit
Put Yo mind at ease!

NO RAVING BEAUTY

Now I'm no raving beauty
And I ain't got no big azz booty
But I have an intellectual mind
And my spirit is divine
I'm conscious and aware
And I love my natural hair
I'm proud of my African roots
And my religion is the truth

I closely gaze at my African ways
I give my ancestors praise
For all the gifts they gave
I look at the color of my eyes
I look at the shape of my thighs
I look at splendor of my skin
I look at the dimple in my chin

I look and wonder if the world can see
How the divine creators showed such favor upon me
And even if not one mention is said
I can see the crown they placed upon my head

Now I'm no raving beauty
And I ain't got no big azz booty
But I have an intellectual mind
And my spirit is divine

BLACK AND BROWN GIRLS

We are nature's masterpieces
From the broadness of our nose
To our beautifully painted toes
From our full pouted lips
To our wide shapely hips
Some will hate us
And some will even try to copy
But the originals are better
And imitations are too sloppy
For so many years
We compared ourselves to
Their standards of beauty
But now they all pay money
To look like yours truly
We went from hot combs
Then To perms
From blowouts
Then To natural curls
We Black and Brown Girls
Are as truthfully precious as pearls
So proudly we will rise
With our heads held high
So, little princess please take your rightful place
Because yours is a beauty to admire
And yours is a beauty to embrace

THE ORIGINAL WOMBMAN

No I'm not just pretty for a Black Girl
Don't you know I'm That Girl?
I'm the Black Mother Pearl
and Damn Right
this is my World
I'm the model of Beauty
I am the Mold
Let the truth be told
I'm the one who gives you
a glorious sight to Behold
I'm a masterpiece that was
designed by the Creator
Tell me where you can find
any woman greater
No I'm not dismayed
By what other may say
Their words fail to mock me
yet they seem too cocky
but when they wish to stand out
I'm the one they Copy
So you see it's indisputable
I am the Original Womb-man
And this is what the world
needs to Over-stand
And I wasn't made by some coincidence
I'm what the universe planned!

BLACK MOTHERS

We was born with a sweet tooth
      for dishing out the Truth
We was born with a firm mother's hand
      to guide the youth
Inside our DNA lies the proof
'Cause we are Black Mothers
      all the way down to our roots

We go about our day teaching not preaching
And even to a child we ain't seen before
      we are an open window to a closed door

She says honey child you don't have to know me
This is my calling so you don't owe me

And yes child
      I can feel your pain
Don't you worry now
      it's a Big Mamma Thang

Something that was left in me long ago
Something that was there when they created my soul

Not meant for you or me to understand
      But I was made to be
      That voice,
      That nudge,
      That comforting hand

And child your future means everything to me
I just wanna open your Eye so that you can see
And there's a reason why glitter trails behind you
You see, that's how the universe
      knows where to find you

So, whether you call yourself a Sun of God or God's Son
    I am the womb that you came from

So, thank y'all for all the Mother's Day praise
    but you're the seeds that we were born to raise

We Black Mothers be
    Home makers
    Care takers
    And don't make me whoop your behind!
    Bad habit breakers

We got too much class
    To be caught up in street fights
    So, we smile real polite
    At folks we don't like
    But we still put it down
    In the bedroom at night

Black mother's
    Make you stand up straight
    Back Talk we don't take
    We teach you to stand out yet still relate
    We make sure you're safe
    And makes sure that you ate
    Everything that we put on that dinner plate

'Cause we ain't the one you wanna play with
And we'll send you outside to get a tree switch
But we can also soothe your soul like calamine lotion on an itch
And we don't throw nothing away we just get it fixed

'Cause we are Black mothers
The cradle rocker of every son,
    daughter, sistah and brotha

You see, we was born with a sweet tooth
      for dishing out the Truth
We was born with a firm mother's hand
      to guide the youth
Inside our DNA lies the proof
'Cause we are Black Mothers
      all the way down to our roots!

BLACK LOVE

Black love is so vital
    yet today we are so insecure
We keep trying to find our way back
    searching for remedies that will reassure

Black love was so treasured
    it was our universal law
It was the thread that kept us connected
    but now we find ourselves too separated
    and too neglected

Black love was so bold
    and so unconcealed
It was a love so divine
    that souls were naturally revealed

Black love was so admired
    our strength was the envy of all
It was our pride and it was our glory
    knowing they could never make us fall

Generations of the past often applauded
    and celebrated their longevity
But today broken homes with single parents
    still carry on but regretfully

Growing up we had relationships to follow
    remember when love was the goal
But today we look back through old scrap books
    wishing we had the past to behold

Love has been lost in youthful minds
      and misplaced by broken hearts
By today's generations who have forgotten
      that making love was really an art

Black love represents the commitment
      to family unification
So let our sons and daughters bare witness
      to telling of this narration

Because our history is what we know
      to be tried and true
And this is how our grandparents
      made it through

Black love is essential
      and we must never allow it to end
So, teach the children their legacy
      for it is our tradition we must defend

NOW
I
SEE

FEAR VS PEACE

Today was not my best day
You know how there are those days
    when it's not just one bad thing
But the kind of day
    when it's one bad thing after the other
I felt like I was I was in the midst of a war
    as if I was executing Kung-Fu inside my head
    blocking and kicking at negative thoughts
    as they charged at me from all directions
Subconsciously I knew that they were after my peace
    so, I searched the corners of my mind
    and I found my peace waiting for me
    saying that we can do this
    and together we can fight those fears
So, we focused on transforming my thoughts
    and replacing my stresses
    with scenes of serenity
Me and my peace began to wage a battle against my fears
    and through my peace I found my strength
It was not going to be easy
    because war never is
But we were fighting for peace
    and defeat is not an option
So, fuck you fear!

BONES IN THE CLOSET

I hear them bones click and clack
I think they got your soul under attack
And that weight on your shoulders
must make life hard to live
I bet if you could turn back time
ain't nothing you wouldn't give
Bet you tired of living
in that perpetual hell
Bet you didn't know
the power of your words
could caste such a treacherous spell

And don't you know that those relics
will steal your peace
And now you can't dream
'cause you can't sleep

But never allow those mistakes
to corrode your space
Don't allow them bones
to seal your fate
For they will sure enough
turn your brown eyes slate
Turn the beat of your heart
in to a fatal heart ache

And I have seen this before
I've seen far worse and more
And If you hold it
You can't breathe
Let it go
So you can grieve
Because your soul will get no reprieve
from this wicked disease

On negativity it will feed
infesting your memories
With fumes so thick
that their stench refuses to leave

You better watch where you step
I think tip toeing might be best
And I think it's time
You laid them bones to rest
Now don't it feel good
To drop that load off your chest
Well if the answer is yes
then go ahead and confess

You see those skeletal remains
from your cold-hearted past
Are leaving a trail of icy artifacts

Yeah, Lady Karma is good for granting
an eye for an eye
And she'll expose those deeds
that you try to deny
She can turn you into a slave
of the ones that you betrayed
And only Lady Karma knows
when your debt has been paid
So, you better gather them bones
and make amends for what you've done
You better clean out your closet
before your soul is none!

THE VALUE OF TIME

All we seem to think about is time
      too much time for this
      and not enough time for that
      time to go to work
      and time to sit and chat
But we waste so much of our time
      when we should cherish our time
For any time that is lost
      is truly the greatest crime
So be mindful of how
      you spend your time
      always place limits on your time
      know the value of your time
      take control of your time
      and never let others waste your time
For time should only be given
      when we decide
      and to whom and why
You see, time is an entity
      that can't be bought
      well at least
      that's what I was taught
But then I thought
      What if time is just a gift?
      And, what if the measurement of time
      is just a myth?
      Would that leave you miffed?
      Well I'll tell you more if you insist
You see our time is priceless
      and no one can place a value on it

But if someone is feeling generous and kind
      then they can give you some of their time

And did you know that too much free time
    can drive some people
    out of their mind
And then they end up
    killing their time
    standing in line
    spending all their nickels
        and dimes
    just for the illusion of
        peace of mind
But I won't let anyone waste my time
    for that would be a tragedy like
    gulping down a bottle of fine wine
    instead of pouring it into a glass
    and taking my sweet time
And don't spend your time
    dwelling on things that tear you up inside
    because most of the time
    it's just all in your mind
    which you would find
    if you took more time
    to relax and unwind
But I won't take up any more of your time
Though I would like to leave you
With these last couple of lines
Never let love leave you blind
Instead pay attention to all of the signs
    because we waste so much of our time
    when we should cherish our time
    for time that is lost
    is truly the greatest crime
So be mindful when you spend time
    place limits on your time
    know the value of your time
    take control of our time
    never let others waste your time

Instead continue to shine
    for your whole life time
    because one day
    we all run out of time

THE DIRTY DIRTY

I'm living in the Dirty, Dirty
Wait, I don't think ya'll hard me
I say I'm living in the Dirty, Dirty
Yeah I don't think they heard me
Where Sistahs be thick and curvy
And Brothas be begging for mercy
But don't try to step up
If you ain't worthy
Yeah these Sistahs gotta a whole lotta Assy
They talk smack 'cause they Sassy
They know how to keep their shit Classy
They say go ahead
      you can get at me
      but let that bullshit pass me
'Cause I'm living in the Dirty, Dirty
Nah, I don't think y'all hard me
Yeah I'm living in the Dirty, Dirty
I don't think they heard me
Here they eat biscuits with Red Eye Gravy
And Old folks be praying for God to save me
People shooting guns at night like they crazy
Them girls be wearing dukes with daisies
Some keep their hair short and wavy
      But out here they be making beautiful babies
Young Brothas might try to play me
      But I'm from Up North
      So that shit don't phase me
Yeah I'm living in the Dirty, Dirty
Nah, I don't think y'all hard me
I say I'm living in the Dirty, Dirty
I don't think they heard me
Here they drink beer straight out the can
And some of those rednecks
Still honor the Klu, Klux, Klan

Their houses decorated with confederate flags
Having kids by their mother's, sister's cousin Roxane
But these gun owner's be hunting man
Spitting tobacco in tin cans
Cooking up moon shine
with pots and pans
and how they got so jacked up
I'll never understand
'Cause I'm living in the Dirty, Dirty
Wait, I don't think y'all hard me
I say I'm living in the Dirty, Dirty
Yeah I don't think they heard me
Now we got this guy named Trump
     Man what a chump
        I think he used to be that kid
        Named Forrest Gump
Now him and Mike Pence
Wanna build up a fence
But I'm just hoping my landlord
Don't increase my rent
'Cause I'm grinding so hard
But that can't even make a dent
Because the Bill money already been spent
So I guess for the next four years
I'll be sipping beers
And working as a part-time cashier at Sears
Collecting Barak Obama souvenirs
Going to Happy Hour cracking jokes
About White House Racketeers
I'm trying not to cry
I'm holding back tears
Watching the rest of the country say cheers
Because as strange as it appears
With Trump they have no fears

And I'm living in the Dirty, Dirty
Nah, I don't think y'all hard me
I said I'm living in the Dirty, Dirty
Damn, I don't think they heard me!

ONE OF BROOKLYN'S FINEST

Now I'm no Rapper
Though sometimes I can dress a little dapper
But they say that I'm nice the way I bestow it
They say I'm the epitome of a poet
And I'm the one you heard about at story telling time
You'll be eating milk and cookies
    While I'm painting pictures across the sky
'Cause I come from the State of
    the New York Knicks
    and the New York Giants
    and I am proud to be known as
    One of Brooklyn's Finest!

I'm one of Brooklyn's finest!
My crown stays lit
    So just call me your royal highness
You see I'm a plus
    And you're just a minus
But when it comes to my people
    I'm very biased
So don't let me have to read you
    Like a book assignment
I'll have your mind locked up
    In solitary confinement
'Cause when I shoot
    I shoot to kill
    And not with kindness
My truth is Dope
    Maybe you should try it
Some say I'm a good looker
And that my mamma taught me how to be a good
    cooker
But later I grew up to be a knowledge pusher
    And now I speak with sub woofers

But when I expanded my consciousness
I became gifted
My soul was lifted
It turned me on like a mental ignition
I developed the skills of poetic technician
    Twisting facts with fiction
    Then my people started to come out and listen

Yeah I'm a laid-back kind of gal
    With a sexy smile
But I'll leave yo azz open
    Like the Panama Canal
I'm good for your soul
    So let me boost your morale
And if you wanna hit me up
    Get at me on PayPal

'Cause I'm stomping bullshit like cockroaches
Learning some lessons from life coaches
And now they got my name on most wanted posters

But please tell me why I see all these young girls
    stressing
Because they boyfriends ain't giving them no
    affection
But then I hear these young boys say
Well If we ain't sexing
    Then we ain't texting

And it seems to me like these days
If you sucking dick
Then you the one they wanna pick
'Cause they ain't looking for a wife
    They just looking for a trick

But just let me spit
Like old school Slick Rick
    The story teller
And I hope that one day
    My book becomes a bestseller
Si Adios Abuela
    I know you like to watch movies like Old Yeller
    But tonight, we'll be spitting lyrics in the downstairs cellar
    So, I think I better go call that DJ fella

'Cause I Live,
I laugh, and I love life
and I ain't going out
    Without a fight

Yeah I keep my circle small
And I'm one of Brooklyn's Finest
My crown stays lit
So just call me your royal highness!

BACK IN MY DAY

They call me the Urban African Flower
      Because I drop wisdom by the hour
I Like my sauce sweet and sour
      But I'm all about that Black Power

I'm something like a freedom fighter
      Disguised as a poetry writer
I keep my headwrap tighter
      Just call me the intellectual delighter

Back in my day
      I was a Nation of Islam Five Percenter
      A poor Project Housing Renter
      Eating beans and rice for dinner
      But I was still born a winner

'Cause Back in My Day
      We mostly had "Black Tokens"
      We use to watch Movies
      With Foxy Brown and Shaft deep stroking
      'Cause they never wanted to show
      Conscious Brothas with their minds open

'Cause back in My Day
      They thought all Black people was lazy
      They thought all the homeless people was just crazy
      Now A lot of my old homies are pushing up daisies
      But having Knowledge of Self is what saved me

'Cause Back in My Day
      I stayed on my grind
      Working at a job Full time

  Clothes shopping at lunch time
  Rushing home to watch Good Times
  Listening to Old School Rhymes
  I thought my Life was sublime

And I knew that I was Fine
  So I Let Brothas pay for my wine
  'Cause you see I was never was a nickel
    looking for a dime
  'Cause If we ain't building
    Then you ain't worth my time

Oh yeah!
  I'm a bullshit detector
  A man erector
  A knowledge injector
  The seed protector

Now they tried to divide us
  To make us weaker
  But I'm still my Brotha and Sistah's Keeper
  And though I spit knowledge like a public speaker
    I'm nothing like a preacher
    'Cause I smoke way too much refer
  But I'm always a truth seeker
  So if you wanna understand my mind
    You gonna have to go deeper

Now they say
  Education creates more opportunity
  But I wish we had less violence in our community
  Because police seem to kill us with impunity
  While The laws are designed to give them immunity

But Back in My Day
    We had more "Black Unity"
    We came together for common goals
    We did what was right for our heart and souls
    But it ain't never too late
        And you ain't never too old
    So let's come together
    And watch our power unfold!

SOCIAL CONSCIOUSNESS

I GOT SOMETHING TO SAY!

I got something weighing heavy on my mind
I got something to say!
I'm not biting my words
Not spitting no blurbs
But I'm shining this light around these curves
    I got something to say!

My 3rd Eye is telling me
That it's time to set you free
And even if I have to take a big rock
And shake that tree
Let the leaves hit the ground
Just make sure you hear the sound
I got something to say!

This weight on me
Is like choke hold on my soul
And I can't rest until this truth be told
Time is moving fast
But I'm not too old
To drop some knowledge
on you righteous souls
I got something to say!

This load is getting heavier each day!
Can't see you how my beloved Ancestors paved the way?
They left us Hieroglyphic symbols and signs

All we have do is understand the meaning
So that we can get the knowledge that we all feening
    I said, I got something to say!

So let's have that conversation
Let's stand in the sun and receive some stimulation
Let's build and pour out some libation
'Cause I got something to say to the Nubian Nation!

BLACK AND BLUE

I am Black
And You are Blue
You see me
And I see you

But I can't imagine
    what you must see
That makes you want to kill
    everyone that looks like me!

But maybe all you can see is
A Drug Dealer
Or some Neighborhood Stealer
A Thug
A Gang Banger
A Prostitute
Or A Pimp
Because you saw the brother walking with a limp!

And you only see the streets with grime
    but you don't see how hard we grind
And now you got lasers locked on me
    like I'm the rotten apple in the tree?
And you don't think I have the right to breathe
    even when I raise my hands and plead

'Cause I'm just Black
    and you are Blue
You have a fear of me
So, I fear from you

And you are the reason
    that I run for my life
    from people like you

'Cause all I can see is
      a protected murderer
      or a selective detective
      Who's threatened by my skin
      wishing that I would just blend in
      and raised to think
      that being Black is a sin
And ready to use deadly force
      because my blackness gave you no choice
Is that's why you pinned me down and silence my voice?

Then you pass judgment on me
      In those cars you drive
        With no intention on saving black lives!

You don't understand my plight!
You don't think I deserve rights!
      But to protect your privilege you will fight!

But I'm still proud to be Black
and it's gonna be hard for you to be Blue
Yet I hope that one day that you will see me
      the way I see you!

MESSAGE VIRAL

Hey y'all,
I sure do hope this message goes Viral
I hope these words tap into your spinal
Send your false perceptions into a spiral
And move wisdom through your soul like a raging tidal

Now don't be alarmed
    This is just a little Black Voodoo
I'm giving you something
    That you're probably not use to
I'm keeping it 100
    I'm not trying to fool you
On the contrary homie
    I'm just trying to school you

Who me?
I'm a proud poetic disciple
And hey thanks for this platform
This Open Mic is quite delightful

I know that some wanna set the trends,
    but I prefer being a classic
And I guess that's kind of rare,
    but I'm cut from a different fabric

And I know some don't understand
    Why it is that we slowly progress
Well the answer is simple
    It's not really that complex
You see we keep spending our money
    While they continue to Invest
We keep thinking checkers
    While they be playing chess

We gotta learn to grow our resources
        And let karma take care of the rest

But the state of Black America
        Has truly become tragic
Bodies are being reconstructed with plastic
Their life styles are becoming too ratchet
And a little too porno graphic
But they need to learn to vibrate higher
        and remove all the static

'Cause showing your Blackness
        is not about representing an image
        it's supposed to be about identifying
        with your African lineage

But we all have a choice to make
        And we can either unify our people
        or watch them emulate
We can either promote self-love
        Or watch our people die with self-hate

But hey,
I sure do hope this message goes Viral
I hope these words tap into your spinal
Send your false perceptions into a spiral
Move wisdom through your soul like a raging tidal

Don't be alarmed
        This is just a little Black Voodoo
I'm giving you something
        That you're probably not use to
I'm keeping it 100
        I'm not trying to fool you
On the contrary homie
        I'm just trying to school you

CHOICES

I stood there
Looking at reflections
    of who I could become
    of who I should become
    and what I can become
But it all depends on me and the choices
    Yeah, those damn choices!
And I hate having the responsibility
    to choose for myself
I hate being the one
    who determines if I will rise or fall
Because I wasn't empowered to think for myself
I was just told to have hope and believe
    and that if I believe
    then blessings I would receive
But now I know that book
    was only meant to control and to deceive
And now I see that I am the one
    who must choose who I can be
Now I see that I am the one who must choose
    who I could become
    who I will become
Now I understand that it all depends on me
    and those choices
Yeah, those damn choices!

FEARSOME TIMES

These are fearsome times that I'm living
Seems no mercy to the poor is being given
Yet those same hypocrites ask to be forgiven
Man, they must think I'm slipping
But that can't be with all this knowledge I'm getting
So, I just fall back and listen
Then I discharge my thoughts from my loaded pen
Striking down men who mockingly offend
I recognize those who may try to pretend
And to those in the struggle my hand I lend

Yet I say again
These are fearsome times we're living in
But I remember when
My surroundings had friends
And I remember when
I was about the age of ten
Tho I didn't understand then
How any other man
Had the upper hand
When it was black people who built this land
Yet it seems as if I stood in the quick sands
Not realizing that this was the master plan

And there are more fearsome times ahead
y'all better get out the bed
'Cause they kill the sleeping heads
They paint these streets red
Their hunger must be fed
And it's time to get the crust out your eyes
Hear the screams and the cries
Learn from the deceit and the history of lies

So that you can understand why
And I'll say it again
These are some fearsome times we're living in

TOO BLACK

They said I was too strong
So they tried to break me
But they failed to realize
It was the universe that made me
They thought I was so easy
So they tried to earn me
But now they understand that
     their sell out money don't concern me
Thought they could slide by saying something slick
Thought they had me trippin with all that bull shyt
They thought I was too loud and too outspoken
But I just woke up from a system that was broken
They said I was too black for them to hire
So I channeled my gifts and became inspired
They said my words are too real
     and sometimes they frighten
I said stop living in fear
     my main purpose is to enlighten
They said that I would fail and that I would never last
But now they just another stepping stone
     living in my past

BLACK LIPS

These enchanted black lips of Kush
Have been passed down to me
From tribes of the African bush

Plump and luscious Lips
Inherited from the kinfolks of ETHIOPIA
One kiss of a Goddess grants Utopia

My Lips are my calling card
From my prominent mouth I'll speak
Cherry Red whispers in the ear of my King
Make these words sound sweet

And when they speak
They say hush
They say come
Sometimes they hum
They say two of me
Is better than one

My lips are sensuously attractive
But beware these semi-glossed plums
Can be most distractive

And they possess so much sway
They merely slither around syllables
These Lips were made for a God
Not for the typical
'Cause the more you intertwine
The more you savor the divine
Yes, I have great offerings inside my kiss
And worthy men will give praise for these black lips

As they chant my ancestor's names

Vocalizing their pain

These Lips smile wide
Because they represent a lineage of pride
Even though at time I use to cry
Because I didn't understand why
My lips were so thick
But now I give honor to my sensual gift
     So, come and let me bless you
With these Black Lips!

BLACK SKIN

Pastors preach and pray
about saving us from our so called sins
But all we hear are crickets
when they're shooting our Black Skin
So, tell me how do we begin
to talk about this deadly beef
'Cause Black Folks in America
ain't safe when it comes to the Police
And pastor can't you see they're committing
cold blooded murder in these streets
then y'all wanna turn around and call for peace
You want us to stop the rioting
and stealing their loot
But nobody listens to us
when we say don't shoot!
And yes we see how the cops get protected
when you know they ain't telling the truth
But it really doesn't matter
because the video camera's got the proof
So, just go on preaching and praying
about our so called sins
because all we hear are Crickets
when they're shooting our Black Skin!

WHAT ABOUT US?

I'm so you glad we have a month of Black History
I'm so glad we have a Dr. King Blvd
and a Malcom-X Street

But tell me why you flood our neighborhoods
      with drugs and liquor stores?
Why do you continue to destroy our black families?
And why do you keep treating our sisters like whores?

Why won't you give us the cure for disease?
Why do you allow poison in our food from overseas?

Why are you killing all the natural land and
      contaminating our water?
Leaving us to die in the hood and not even call it a slaughter

But allow me to ask a few more questions
      if I may be so bold
What about all the lies that have been told?

What about all the books that have been burned?
What about all the lessons we never learned?

What about all the lives that were enslaved?
What about taking the truth to your corpse grave?

What about all the warriors we've lost
      to keep our past alive?
What about all we have forgotten?
Stolen pieces of time!

FAKE DEMOCRACY

Don't live by their rules
Make your own rules
You better grab your net
And catch these jewels
Because our vote is pointless
In their rigged election pool
Can't you see we look like fools
In this is fake democracy
Indoctrinated by their schools
Our struggles will not end
In this system we can never win
With no regards for the fire within
We've become disheartened by the devil's grin
Then they shun us like sin
Because we were born with black skin

But we have enemies outside looking in
Looking for our weakness so they can do us in
But here we are as divided as ever
And the powers that be still think their clever
But our votes ain't for sale
      not now
      not ever
So, let's take pride in this defense
Time is valuable so be mindful of how it's spent
Conceive your plan to stay one step ahead
And focus on your own goals instead

So never live by their rules
Make your own rules
You better grab your net
And catch these jewels
Because our vote is pointless
In their rigged election pool

Can't you see we look like fools
In this is fake democracy
Indoctrinated by their schools
Our struggles will not end
In this system we can never win
With no regards for the fire within
We've become disheartened by the devil's grin
Then they shun us like sin
Because we were born with black skin

IDENTITY STOLEN

It's amazing how you criticize the darkness of our
    complexions
Is that because you fail to realize our ancestor's
    resurrection
Classifying our skin as dark or light
Choosing who you consider to be Black or White
Making fun of our big lips and the shape of our azz
Deciding who you tear down and who you let pass
Degrading our culture if we want to wear
head wraps, dreds or braids
But still don't want to give us credit for all the
    inventions
And contributions we've made

It was you who took away our identity
And then gave us your names
But it seems like the more we progress
The more things stay the same
And when our leaders try to lead
It's your bullets that make them bleed
And it really wasn't that long ago
That you hung us from trees

And now you want us to keep us dancing
To the beat of your drum
Telling us we should blend in
But have you forgotten
Where we came from
But this you can't deny
For this is our truth
Black skin is the beginning
And Black skin will always be the root

WORLD OF "INSTAGRAM"

Hey Fam!
    It seems like we're living in a world of
    "Instagram"
    And I know all these Women getting famous
        off their Hair and Booty Glam
    But I'm just out here to let you know who I am
    And I came to drop some knowledge about
        the Black Fam
    And maybe shed some light on
        the enemy's plan
    Because the power is in our hands
        So, I hope I reach a few
        conscious folks who inner-stand

Sometimes I'm just surfing the Web at home
        sitting in my pajamas
'Cause hey, I don't want no bad vibes
        coming back on me like karma
And yeah we laugh at jokes about
        Primadonna's
        Human Piranhas
        And baby mamas
        Who sometimes create their own drama

But I can't believe how I many people going crazy
    for those plastic girls
    With fake assets and fake curls
    I just shake my head and asked myself
        What happened to this world?

And It's so sad but
    I see some people that be ignorant as fuck
    And still out here just trying to make a buck

And I see some people so selfish and greedy
    And still be trying to pimp donations
        from the needy
    And I pause like really?
    I know y'all can feel me!

So, I just stay in my lane and speak my truth
    And I sincerely hope that these words
        reach the youth
    But please pass me with your opinions unless
        you got some proof

Because you won't ever see me
    getting caught up in those
    Fake pastors or puppet masters
    Trying to turn my life into a sad disaster

'Cause they just trying to throw me curves
    But I can hit them like I'm a batter
    while I'm steady reaching new levels
    On a Spiritual ladder

SPIRITUAL AWAKENING

RESTORATION OF MY SOUL

I've come to the ocean of my soul
In pursuit of a resurrection
Where I am embracing my imperfections
Learning some lessons
And shedding some light on the blessings

I came to conquer my struggles
Knowing that day to day I must keep on pressing
I came here because it's time for me to stop stressing
Time to master myself
     I must stand
     Even if I stumble
     Time to fight
     I must claim my power
     But stay humble

My spirit still speaks with confusion
So I sit in silence to find the solutions
I may have to walk
But I'm not alone
'Cause I follow the light of my ancestor's home
I seek the still waters
And I travel the steepest mountains
To drink from an enlightened fountain

I'm needing some restoration
     Needing some fillings
        in the cracks of my foundation
I am whole but not yet complete
There are still some levels that I'm afraid to compete
Because I keep failing to realize that I'm the elite
But the bands on this mediocre existence
     have been broken

And this new life got me open
Now compelling me to move my feet
To follow that which makes me strong
And leave that which makes me weak

I came to the ocean of my soul
In pursuit of a resurrection
Where I'm embracing my imperfections
Learning some lessons
And shedding some light on the blessings

WHO AM I

Who am I?
I'm a beam of light
A direct projection
The sun and the moon
Gave me my direction

I'm the matter existing in time and space
I'm energy that cannot be destroyed or erased

I'm the essence moving through matter
You can't stop me
To those who doubt me
I say just watch me

I'm the sun in your eye
I'm the answer to your why
I'm the beat in your dance
I'm the flame in romance

I'm the fruit from the tree
I'm the honey from the bee
I'm the cinnamon in your spice
I'm the day in your night

I'm the darkness in your light
I'm the wrong in your right
I'm the song in your ear
I'm the truth that you fear

I'm the corner of your mind
I'm the vision for the blind
I'm the melanin in your skin
I'm the place where you begin

I'm the yin to your yang
I'm the pleasure in your pain
I'm the joy in your laugh
I'm the future to your past

I'm the seed in your womb
I'm the air that you consume
I'm the wisdom in your words
I'm your degree to the 3rd

I am the salt
That flavors the sea
I am you
And you are me!

ILLUSION OF PERFECTION

Perfection is just an illusion
That I chase in my dreams
Until the day that my dreams
Become my reality

So, this flower that I hold in my hand
Symbolizes my higher self
In that I grow as it grows
And I thrive as it thrives

So, I give it the water of my thoughts
And the sunlight of my knowledge
And I let it grow inside of me
The earth
Nurturing it
Attending to its needs
Until it bears fruit
In such an abundance
That I may drink it like wine
Quenching my minds thirst

Meditating on my thoughts
As they come in to fruition
Because my reason for being
Is not simply just to be
But to grow and thrive for a purpose

So, these are the words that I say slowly each day
In my daily affirmations
In my meditations
Even in the mist of my orgasmic stimulations
Until it becomes a manifestation

Like the illusion of perfection
That I chase in my dreams
Until the day that my dreams
Become my reality

COSMIC PERCEPTIONS

A vision has consumed me
Majestic energy moving through me

Arousing cosmic perceptions
Igniting astral projections

Imagining the unimaginable
Fathoming the unfathomable

Extracted the mental illusions
No more false conclusions

Linking me to other dimensions
Facilitating outer body extensions

Clarity illuminating my path
Reaching my higher self at last

Taking away fear and giving me peace
Eliminating doubt and disbelief

Seeing my existence in true form
Now my reality is no longer the norm

Filling my spiritual void with abundance
I am a reflection of the universe my oneness

Now understanding my place
In the confines of this human race

Allowing me to see through my mind's eye
So that my spirit can finally fly!

SEEING BEYOND 20-20

My mind's eye has emerged!
No I ain't joking that's my word!
    And these new lenses ain't even funny
No I ain't talking about no 20-20
    'Cause this sight is worth more than money
So now I'm gonna have to dismiss you
    Yes, your chaos is has been refused
    'Cause I can't be misused
    With these new x-ray views
Yeah go ahead and take a minute
    'Cause you seem confused
And I'm so grateful for this 3rd sight
    that I've been given
And now I'm loving life
    now I'm finally living
And my mind's eye is guiding me
    with such precision
It's navigating me beyond
    the ordinary vision
And it's really kind of sad
    That you ain't got a clue
    About what this 3rd eye can do
But all you really need to know is that
    I can see right through you Boo!

THE GOD'S CHILD

For centuries
    they have tried to block me and stop me
Sometimes they lift me up
    just so they can drop me
    to the ground
They tried to stifle my words
    they said hush
    don't make a sound!
Then they fall back and smile
    but all the while
    they forgot about one thing
    I am the God's Child!
So, you're thinking that I'm some featherweight
    that you can dominate
    but, you just wait
Because the God in me will radiate
With all the spiritual food I get
    from my ancestors when I meditate
And when you try to divide us with words
    I study truth so that I can debate
And if you try to block my path ahead
    I'll just exit through the side gate
Because every time you try to do me in
    I'll eat that shit up like vitamins
    because you're giving me insight to things
    that I didn't know then
And yes, I'm more than aware
    that you've got this system on lock
So, that's why I don't even bother to call the cops
But if it's my time to go
    then it's also my time to shine
And one day you will know the truth
    when my greatness leaves you blind
    And when my people come!

    there will be a hundred of them
    to your one
    heed my words son
    my wrath has just begun
And then you will know that you can never
    stop the God's Child
Unless you are ready to walk
    your last fucking mile!

ANCIENT WINDS

Now you may not understand my significance
    because your arrogance leads you to believe
    that my existence is inconsequential
And you may not want to acknowledge my presence
    But, yet I'm here in the midst of your air
    watching you breathe
    as you come to concede
    in your tortured reality
For I am part of the ancient winds
    Empowered by my divinity within
    Allowing me to become one with the wind
    Enabling me to shift and blend in
    With the spirit of my Kin
 Yes, my Kin folks
    Holding my place at the table
    Leaving me a plate to eat
    When I am able
As my gift of intuition
    turns into premonitions
    of spirits in transitions
They are drawn to my soul
    like an accessible admission
I see them as visions
Like exquisite paintings
On a canvas in my head
    adorned by the shadows of brilliant reds
I see the beauty of all their hues
I see the ocean in the midst
    of their heavenly Blues
I see them with my mind's eye
    where nothing is unseen
I see the Continent of Africa
    in the shades of green

So, you may not understand my significance
        because your arrogance leads you to believe
        that my existence is inconsequential
And you may not want to acknowledge my presence
But, yet I'm here
In the midst of your air
And I ain't going nowhere!

WOKE

CONFESSIONS

Why do I still feel the need to make these confessions
    Like I'm still trying to shed some old sins
    Like butterflies shed their caterpillar skin
    Like these are demons that I've already cleansed

And I can't help it if some don't comprehend
    the way that I fornicate with my pen
    maybe that's why I keep coming back
    to give it to you again

And it doesn't matter if you be my foe or friend
    because this is my own obsession
    so, just let me purge
    these words again

Let me stand here and spout
    because I need to cast out
    any remaining insecurities or doubts
    and if you didn't come in peace
    then I respectfully say
    get the fuck out!

'Cause I didn't ask you for your permission
    and this ain't about no damn competition
So, when I fail to recognize my own reflection
    then I know it's time for me to
    fight this depression

'Cause I do this for myself
    and not for your blessings
So, who are you to judge me?
    well I'm just asking a question

And I suppose there are others like me
    well maybe I'm just guessing
But never the less
    I'm gonna give you this message

So, can you hear these words that I speak
    from my sober beak
Because closed minds
    may sometimes be too weak

And when night time falls
    I'm still gone walk these streets
    In search of a microphone waiting for me

In some dark enchanted room
    Where all but one light has been consumed
    Where I come to get some release
    Where I come to speak my peace
    Where I tell the bartender no thank you please
    You see, I come from a different type of creed

So, just let me roll up my sleeves
    so, I can let these words bleed
    'cause a good old confession is all I really need!

FUCK MEDIOCRITY

Fuck being mediocre!
Because conformism is one of the greatest crimes
      against our humanity
And why should anyone settle for being ordinary?
When we were meant to be extraordinary?

And when did having a life of savorless events
      filled with meaningless encounters
      become so routine?

When did being similar become the norm?
And when did we lose that desire to be great?

When did we start declining to reach our full potential?
Has this new reality reprogrammed our minds?
Are we just an imitation of life?
Because it seems that we are no longer striving
To be the magnificent beings that we were created to be

Are we settling for a carefree journey
      rather than the triumphant battle?

Can we only grasp the shades within the lines?
Are we too afraid to venture outside the box?

Because it seems that the gift of imaginations
      Are going to waste
And we have become a sea of captured minds
Minds that cease to reach beyond the limits of the sky
Minds that are just quietly waiting to die

When did we become the sheep
      with our heads buried in the grass?
Has my biggest fear come to pass?

      Is this new way of life here to last?
So I ask, wouldn't you rather be enigma
      rather than an easy read?

Let me release your rage
Let me rattle your cage
So that you can find the path
      that you were meant to blaze
And break you out of that comfort zone
      Because this life is yours to own

Because fuck being mediocre!
For conformism is one of the greatest crimes
      against our humanity
And why should anyone settle for being ordinary?
When we were meant to be extraordinary?

I DO THIS FOR MY PEOPLE

For my people, for my people
I'm gonna do this for my people
I'm gonna go hard for my people
I'm gonna spit these barz for my people
I'm gonna get lit for my people
I'm gonna raise this fist for my people
I'm gonna drop knowledge for my people
I'm gonna pay homage to my people
Damn right I'm gonna holla for my people
I'm gonna spend black dollars with my people
I'm gonna bring hope to my people
I'm gonna stay Woke for my people
Elevate minds for my people
Keep folks in line for my people
I'm gonna spit truth for my people
Kick ass like Bruce for my people
I'm gonna make plans with my people
Give my right hand to my people
Build foundations with my people
Pour out libation with my people
I'm gonna be in sync with my people
Be wise and think with my people
I'm gonna use my art for my people
I'm gonna give my heart to my people
You know I'm gonna fight for my people
I'm gonna shine this light for my people
I'm gonna never gonna lie to my people
I'm gonna open my 3rd Eye for my people
I'm gonna go the mile for my people
I might get hostile for my people
I'm gonna make noise for my people
I'm gonna raise my voice for my people
Always on point with my people
I'm gonna smoke this joint with my people

I'm gonna talk the talk for my people
I'm gonna walk the walk for my people
I'm gonna give props to my people
Never trust these cops for my people
I'm gonna bring peace to my people
I'm gonna protest in these streets for my people
I'm gonna be down for my people
I'm gonna wear my crown for my people
Yeah, I'm gonna be a queen for my people
'Cause I have a dream for my people!

FOR THE R.B.G.
(The Red, Black and Green Flag)

<u>You say</u>:   Oh beautiful for spacious skies
<u>And I say</u>: For the Red, for the Black and the Green
<u>You say</u>:   For purple mountain majesties
        Oh, how I wish this was all just a bad dream
<u>And I say</u>: And you think racism ain't really as bad it seems?

So, tell me why
Should I
Pledge an allegiance to the flag
Of the United States of the former slave masters
Because I've had enough of that
and as a matter of fact
I now pledge my allegiance to the R.B.G.
Standing with those who love me for me
Red - For the blood of the ancestors
Black - For the awakening of a Black Nation
And green - For the mother land
That you raped!
Must I demonstrate?

Hey America!
Why should God shed his grace on thee?
Yes, I mean seriously
Don't you remember the way you hung
our ancestors from trees
with no attempt for reparations to make amends
How could that possibly be?

But your God ain't my God
so, let's get that straight
because your God allowed

black people to be slaves
must I explain?

You see, my God lives deep inside
and your God lives apart from you
up in the sky
And my God empowers me to see
while your God leaves us blind
and dependent upon thee

My country tis of thee
Sweet land of misery
Of thee I sing!
Land where my ancestors died
Land of false pride
From every mountain side
So help me God, let the truth ring

Because mine eyes have seen the glory
and we have awakened from this bullshit story
that you taught me
and now you try to teach it to our seeds

This country has taken everything from me
and yet we still bleed
because you just won't leave us be
and let us truly be free!

<u>So, you</u>
<u>Continue to say:</u>   Oh beautiful for spacious skies
<u>And I say</u>: For the Red, for the Black and the Green
<u>You say</u>:   For purple mountain majesties
     Oh, how I wish this was all just a bad dream
<u>And I say:</u> And you think racism ain't really as bad it
     seems?

MY TRUTH IS DOPE

Watch all these lies fall off
As I inhale and puff
This time I'm calling your bluff
'Cause I've lived in this cloud of confusion long enough

Some days I write poems to read
And some days I write poems to spit
And sometimes I just roll these seeds
    Of wisdom into a spliff
As I Anticipate the buzz off the hit
Then into a higher state of consciousness I drift
Exhaling all your mental tricks
Damn, my truth is so Legit!

So pass me with those lies
'Cause I rather stay woke
But you can get a hit of my truth
Go ahead and take a toke
And watch all those lies go up in smoke
My truth has got me so high
My truth is so dope
I inhale so much haze that sometimes I choke
And if it gets too thick I can snort it like coke
While I'm steady taking notes
With the tip of my pen I stroke, and I stroke

Okay wow, I think I got you on the ropes
Yeah, I felt this truth hit you in the back of your throat
I hope you can comprehend the depths of my scope
Because the truth is my religion
And I'm spreading it like I was the Pope!

TRUTH PILL

I know that the truth can be a hard pill to swallow
But swallow we must
Because some of us don't know
     who we really are

Some of us don't understand
     All the destruction put upon us
     And the merciless slaughter
     Of generations of our sons and daughters

So, I it's time to take this truth pill
     With a tall glass of water
     Don't worry if you can't afford a doctor
     This is tabs on me
     You know I got you
     I got the prescription
     For your mental affliction

I'll cover the Bill
     I'll give you unlimited refills
     Because It's time for us to take
     This Truth Pill

Take it as needed
     And each dose must be completed
     Now there may be some side affects
     Because knowing the truth
     Is gone make you upset
     But don't worry
     It's okay
     Just take that pill every day
     Until that apathy goes away

Because all their lies
    Are what's killing our lives
    Leaving you blind
    And always two steps behind
    With a conditioned mind

Sorry but I'm gone have to let this knowledge slap ya
    Because the Truth is what we after
    So please wake up and
    Let this reality rap-ya
    And never mind those
    Black Churches and Black Pastors
    'Cause you are your own master

This pill will erase all those old bad habits
    So, just free your mind
    And let your soul catch it
    Yeah, we know the awakening is gone be
        problematic
    That's why when the see you learning the truth
    They start to Panic
    Because changing your perspective
    Is gonna cause some havoc
    And when it comes to the truth
    I'm the pusher and the addict

So, don't worry if you can't afford a doctor
    This is tabs on me
        And you know I got you
    I got the prescription
        For your mental affliction
    I'll cover the Bill
    I'll give you unlimited refills
    Because It's time for us to take this Truth Pill!

HELLA FOCUSED

I'm Hella, Hella focused
Spitting these Barz like
      Supercali-Fragilistic-Expialidocious
Keep your family and friends the closest
Now prepare for the wrath
      of the Conscious Black Lotus
My wordplay is ferocious
Your false tongue smells like halitosis
Your wickedness is atrocious
I'm unleashing knowledge,
      but the truth must be taken in doses

We know slavery almost broke us
We know the KKK still wanna rope us
We know the police wanna smoke us
But, Oh Happy Day!
      Because Knowledge of Self Woke Us!

Yeah, I'm Hella, Hella focused
Spitting these Barz like fuck your hypnosis!
No more Hocus Pocus
We know your history is bogus
'Cause our ancestors told us!

No, GMO's can't grow this
No, most people can't flow this
My words hit like grenades, so I gotta throw this
Now stand back cause I'm about to blow this!
And I'm blessed because I know this

      I say I'm Hella, Hella focused
Spitting these Barz for my people
So glad that I wrote this
Shining my light, so glad I spoke this

I'm manifesting power
Your mind just stopped!
Because I froze it
I paused to take a hit,
      and that joint is fat because I rolled it
Yeah you lost this case is over because I closed it
And I hope you share this piece, so I can promote it

I say I'm Hella, Hella focused got damn it!
And to my people I hope you can understand it
Remember that peace comes when you demand it
And If they see you winning your haters can't stand it
Your thoughts were too small, so I had to expand it
I see you waking up because that's the way I planned it
I'm flying too high, so I guess it's time to land it
'Cause first I write the Poetry
      Then I grab the Mic and I slam it!

THE TRUTH

Just give me the truth
    But hold the cranberry juice
'Cause I want that straight Absolute
    Yeah, keep it 100 Proof

Give me that truth non-polluted
Give it to me deeply rooted and undisputed

Give it to me without the sugar coat
I wanna hear it straight from Malcom-X throat
    And Harriet Tubman quotes
I wanna read it from library notes
    And from great leaders who spoke
This ain't no joke
    This is about being Woke!

Give me the truth for real
    The truth they conceal
Give me the truth
    That time will reveal
Just give me the dang truth!
I want the lies exposed
    All the information disclosed
I want you tell it like it is
    so I can handle my biz

Because the truth is what I'm looking for
    Yeah, give me the maximum dose
    Pure, uncut and raw
I want it stripped down
    Like hardwood floors
Let me hear it loud
    Like cops knocking down my door

Listen to me Son!
Some spit just for fun
Some run from the light
    But I thrive in the Sun
Some blind sheep
Are still asleep
'Cause they scared to eat
    But I ain't that one
I'd rather feel the pain
    Then be doped up and numb
And if you slept on me
    Then you must be dumb

'Cause there's a reality
    That some of you
    Are too blind to see
Yeah, I'm woke as I can be
    I have a Consciousness Degree

So, give it to me right and exact
    Yeah, I want the unshakable matter of fact
I want my brain locked loaded and strapped
    'Cause once you wake up you can't go back!

www.ingramcontent.com/pod-product-compliance
Lightning Source LLC
Chambersburg PA
CBHW060813050426
42449CB00008B/1646